SKATEBOARDING

BY JOHN HAMILTON

A&D Xtreme
An imprint of Abdo Publishing | www.abdopublishing.com

Visit us at
www.abdopublishing.com

Published by Abdo Publishing Company, a division of ABDO, PO Box 398166, Minneapolis, Minnesota 55439. Copyright ©2015 by Abdo Consulting Group, Inc. International copyrights reserved in all countries. No part of this book may be reproduced in any form without written permission from the publisher. A&D Xtreme™ is a trademark and logo of Abdo Publishing Company.

Printed in the United States of America, North Mankato, Minnesota.
052014
092014

Editor: Sue Hamilton
Graphic Design: Sue Hamilton
Cover Design: John Hamilton
Cover Photo: Corbis
Interior Photos: Alamy-pgs 12-13 & 14; AP-pgs 1, 2-3, 19 (bottom), 21 (inset), 22, 23 (right top & bottom), 24-25, 30-31 & 32; Brian McStotts-pg 7; Corbis-pgs 10-11, 16-17, 18, 20-21, 23 (left), 26-27 & 27 (inset); Getty Images-pgs 4-5, 6, 6 (inset), 15, 19 (top) & 28-29; Glow Images-pg 9 (bottom); Thinkstock-pgs 8 & 9 (top); Wikimedia/Pundi-pg 31.

Websites
To learn more about Action Sports, visit booklinks.abdopublishing.com. These links are routinely monitored and updated to provide the most current information available.

Library of Congress Control Number: 2014932224

Cataloging-in-Publication Data

Hamilton, John.
 Skateboarding / John Hamilton.
   p. cm. -- (Action sports)
 Includes index.
 ISBN 978-1-62403-443-5
 1. Skateboarding--Juvenile literature.   I. Title.
 796.22--dc23

                                                     2014932224

CONTENTS

SKATEBOARDING

A skateboard is just a board on wheels, but expert skaters turn it into a trick-filled ride filled with speed and danger. They take their outrageous blend of balance and skills and face off against the monster known as gravity.

Skateboarders often fall, but they get back up and try again. With practice, skaters push past "it can't be done" and enter the realm of "I did it!"

HISTORY

Skateboarding began in the 1940s and 1950s when kids attached roller skate wheels to boards and wooden crates.

In the 1960s, California surf shops produced mini-surfboards with wheels. Surfers bought these early skateboards to help them practice when they couldn't go out on the waves. Skateboards helped with balance and were fun. But they were dangerous. The wheels broke and boards were difficult to control.

California skater Patti McGee performs a handstand in 1965.

In the 1970s, both the wheels and the boards improved. The first concrete skateparks opened in California and Florida in 1976. The sport became an official event in ESPN's X Games in 1995.

Skater Bob Jarvis tries out the bowl at the Carlsbad Skate Park in California in the 1970s. Carlsbad first opened in 1976.

Xtreme Fact:
Skateboarding was first called "sidewalk surfing."

BOARDS

The part that skateboarders stand on is called the deck. It is usually made of maple wood. Skateboarders choose between shortboards and longboards, depending on what they want to do.

A SHORTBOARD is used for tricks. Being short and lightweight, it is easier to move and get off the ground.

Deck
The wooden board on which a skater stands.

Wheel

Wheels vary in size, color, and material. Larger diameter wheels are used for speed and a smooth ride. Smaller wheels weigh less and are on boards used for tricks.

Mounting Bolts
The hardware used to mount the truck to the board.

Truck
The metal axel on which the wheels are mounted.

A shortboard is 30 to 32 inches (76 to 81 cm) long and 7 to 8 inches wide (18 to 20 cm).

Longboards are about 30 to 40 inches (76 to 102 cm) long and 12 inches wide (30 cm).

A *LONGBOARD* is used for cruising (riding on the streets) and carving (making long, wide turns).

SAFETY EQUIPMENT

Skateboarding is a dangerous sport. Broken bones, sprained wrists, scraped-off skin, bruises, chipped teeth, and concussions have always been a risk for skaters. Helmets, together with elbow and knee pads, plus gloves and wrist guards, help protect skaters. Skateboarding pits humans against gravity, and gravity often wins.

Xtreme Quote: "Lost my board...I twanked my knee. Both knees are twanked. Wrist. My wrist is danked. Twanked and danked... Is there anything that doesn't look like it's hurt?"
-Skateboarder on the 1987 film The Search for Animal Chin

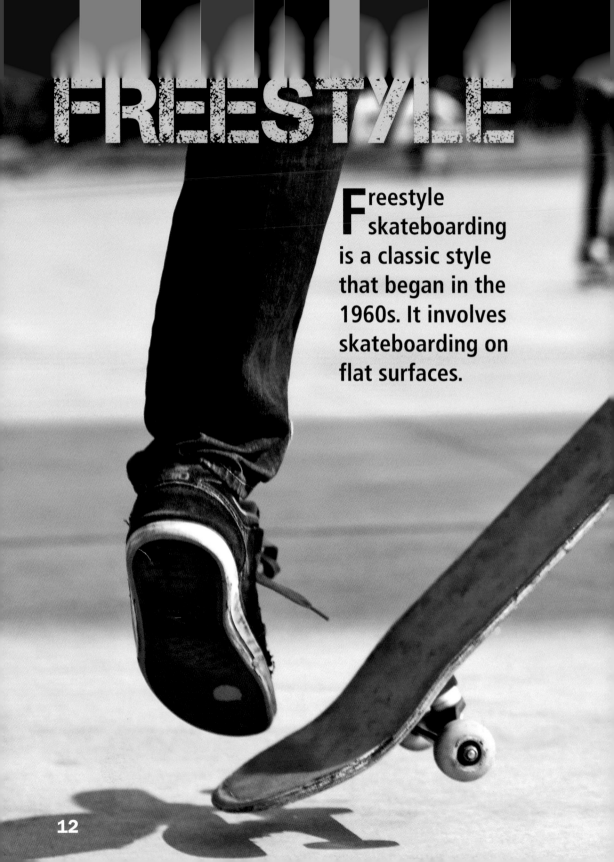

FREESTYLE

Freestyle skateboarding is a classic style that began in the 1960s. It involves skateboarding on flat surfaces.

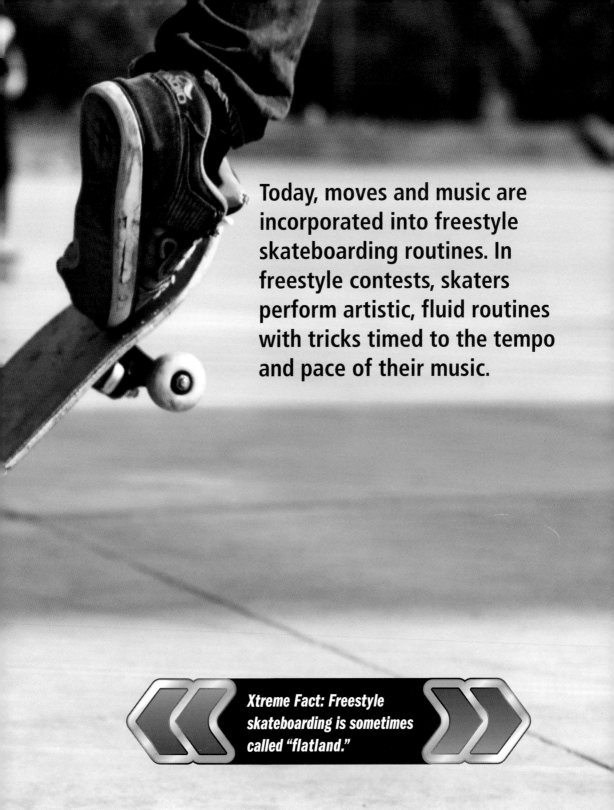

Today, moves and music are incorporated into freestyle skateboarding routines. In freestyle contests, skaters perform artistic, fluid routines with tricks timed to the tempo and pace of their music.

Xtreme Fact: Freestyle skateboarding is sometimes called "flatland."

FREESTYLE TRICKS

Freestyle tricks are performed on the top, bottom, sides, front, and back of a skateboard.

Freestyle skater Kilian Martin performs a handstand.

Freestyle skaters are acrobats with cred. Top skaters master such tricks as the 50/50 spin, pogo, fan flip, sidewinder, wrap-around, casper, broken fingers, and truckstand.

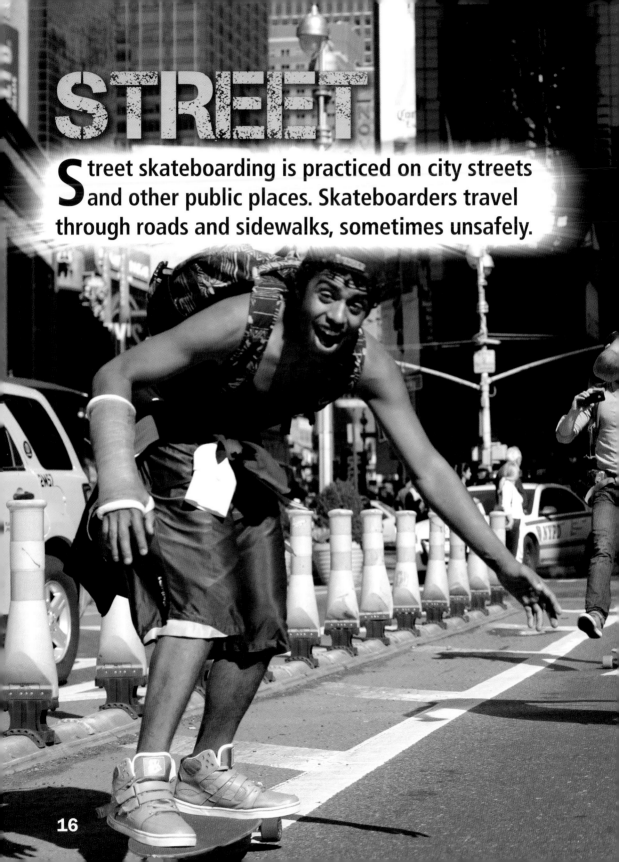

STREET

Street skateboarding is practiced on city streets and other public places. Skateboarders travel through roads and sidewalks, sometimes unsafely.

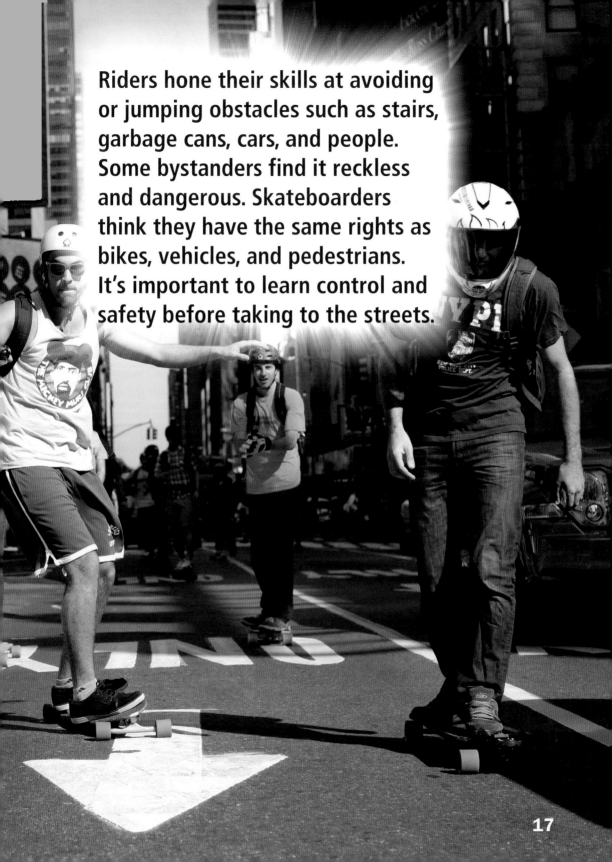

Riders hone their skills at avoiding or jumping obstacles such as stairs, garbage cans, cars, and people. Some bystanders find it reckless and dangerous. Skateboarders think they have the same rights as bikes, vehicles, and pedestrians. It's important to learn control and safety before taking to the streets.

STREET TRICKS

Obstacles found in cities are used for street skateboarding tricks. Ollies, primos, slides, and flips help skaters move across railings, over curbs, and around objects. These obstacles are known as "street furniture."

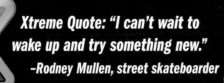

Xtreme Quote: "I can't wait to wake up and try something new."
–Rodney Mullen, street skateboarder

VERT

Vert skateboarding takes place on a vertical surface. It is also called ramp skating. Vert began with skaters riding the walls of empty pools during a drought in California in the 1970s. Today, vert skaters roll on carefully crafted half-pipe ramps that are 14 to 15 feet (4.3 to 4.6 m) tall. Using shortboards, skaters achieve fast speeds, gain great air, and perform dangerous tricks.

Rob Lorifice performs in a
vert competition.

VERT RAMPS

Coping

Table

Vert

Transition

Flat

WOODWARD

WOODWARD

WOODWARD

VERT TRICKS

Vert tricks are performed on half-pipes, quarter-pipes, or bowls. Skaters drop from a ramp and gain speed. Tricks are either aerial, where the skater is airborne, or lip tricks, where the skater balances on the edge of the ramp, or "lip." Popular aerial tricks, or "airs," include grabs and rotations, such as 360s (one full rotation around, or 360 degrees). Lip tricks include stalls, pivots, rock and rolls, and handplants.

Tony Hawk slides a rail at the 2003 X Games.

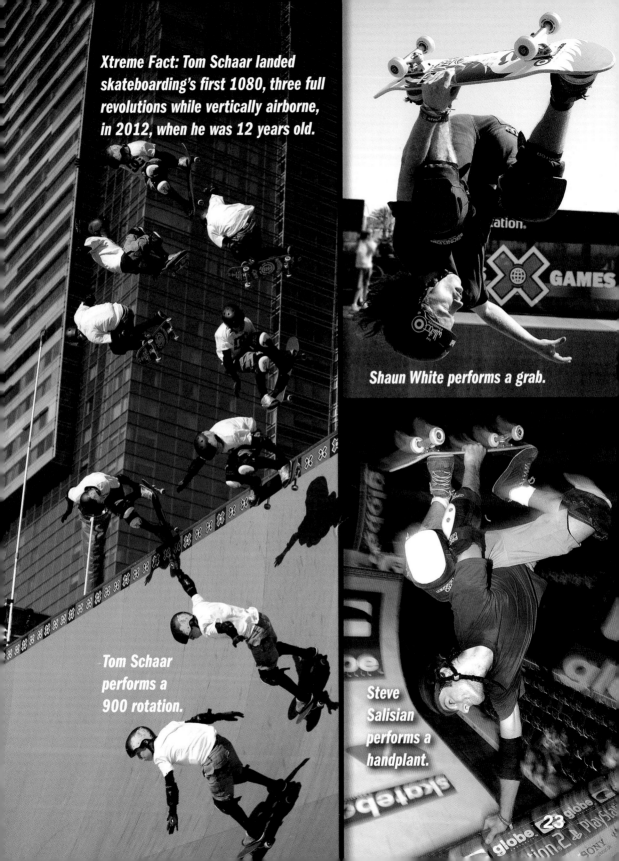

Xtreme Fact: Tom Schaar landed skateboarding's first 1080, three full revolutions while vertically airborne, in 2012, when he was 12 years old.

Shaun White performs a grab.

Tom Schaar performs a 900 rotation.

Steve Salisian performs a handplant.

DOWNHILL

Downhill skateboarding is a wild, dangerous rip down paved roads. It features high hills or mountains, hairpin turns, blind curves, and speeds topping 80 mph (129 kph).

Xtreme Quote: *"It's a form of survival because that's the bottom line... survival."*
-Ethan Lau, downhill skateboarder

At such high speeds, downhill skateboarding is extremely dangerous. Skaters must have excellent balance and be daring. Downhill skateboarding can be illegal if not performed on a closed course.

Kevin Reimer rips downhill on his longboard.

BIG AIR

ig air skaters take 35-inch (89-cm) -long skateboards down a megaramp. This is a three-section extreme challenge featuring a roll-in, a gap jump, and a vert quarter-pipe. The 40- to 197-foot (12- to 60-m) roll-in allows skaters to build up speed to cross the gap.

Andy Macdonald skates the big air ramp at the 2006 X Games.

The gap varies in length from 25 to 70 feet (7.6 to 21 m). The final quarter-pipe section may be 18 feet (5.5 m) tall. It is used to slow down skaters, or to allow them to perform a vert trick before completing the run.

X GAMES

The Summer X Games feature skateboard vert, skateboard park, street league skateboarding, and big air skateboarding competitions.

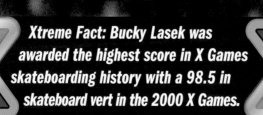

Xtreme Fact: Bucky Lasek was awarded the highest score in X Games skateboarding history with a 98.5 in skateboard vert in the 2000 X Games.

The games are broadcast each year by ESPN. Many of the world's best men and women skaters come to compete. Skateboarding legend Tony Hawk, a longtime competitor in the X Games, is also an announcer.

GLOSSARY

Carving
A wide, smooth turn on a skateboard where all four wheels remain in contact with the riding surface. Or, in an aerial stunt, to travel in a smooth arc.

Concussion
A severe blow to the head that injures the brain and may cause confusion or a temporary loss of consciousness.

Cred
Credibility. Worthy of respect.

Cruising
A smooth, easy ride on the streets, usually on a longboard.

Deck
The flat surface on which a skateboarder stands.

ESPN
A television network that broadcasts entertainment and sports programming.

Gravity

The force that pulls a body toward the center of the Earth.

Half-Pipe

A large, U-shaped ramp used to perform jumps and tricks by such athletes as skateboarders.

Megaramp

A large vert ramp used by skateboarders and bicycle motocross (BMX) racers.

Ollie

A jump performed without a ramp. The skater places his or her back foot down on the tail (back) of the board. That force brings the board off the ground.

Quarter-Pipe

A ramp that is half the size of a half-pipe. It is used to perform jumps and tricks.

Rail

A metal surface, such as a handrailing, that a skateboarder jumps onto and slides down its length.

X Games

Extreme sporting events, such as skateboard competitions, that are broadcast each year in the summer and winter by the ESPN television network.

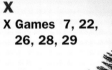